ATYPICAL ANOREXIA NERVOSA

A Compassionate Guide to Understanding, Recognizing, and Breaking Free from the Unseen Eating Disorder in Children and Adults

By

Gretel C. McGuffin

Copyright @2024

TABLE OF CONTENT

CHAPTER ONE.................................7

What is Anorexia?.................7

Types of Anorexia.................11

Psychological Characteristics of Anorexia 15

CHAPTER TWO.................................18

Atypical Anorexia.................18

Traits Associated with Atypical Anorexia 23

CHAPTER THREE.................................31

Unusual Manifestations of Anorexia Nervosa 31

Indicators to Monitor.................37

CHAPTER FOUR.................................40

Difficulties Posed by Atypical
Anorexia 40

Adverse Effects of Atypical
Anorexia 46

CHAPTER FIVE...................................52

Treatment for Atypical Anorexia ...52

Recovery from Atypical Anorexia..60

CHAPTER SIX...................................64

Treatment for Eating Disorders in
Individuals with Elevated Body
Mass...................................64

END...................................73

Atypical anorexia nervosa or "the Unseen Eating Disorder as I prefer to call it, is a condition in which the individual exhibits the characteristic signs and symptoms of anorexia nervosa. Nevertheless, their weight consistently falls within or above the medically established range for optimal health. Due to persons with Atypical anorexia not falling under the underweight category, clinicians may face difficulties in promptly identifying the disorder, which presents substantial obstacles in terms of diagnosis and therapy. Atypical anorexia is difficult to identify as it is characterized by a normal weight and masked by outward happiness. Individuals with this condition often face prejudice in healthcare settings and receive messages that downplay their illness. They may be encouraged to restrict their food intake, follow trendy diets, or engage in excessive exercise, which further undermines their well-being.

Due to the common association of "thin" with "healthy," crucial chances to detect, confront, and manage this eating problem frequently go unnoticed. If you are constantly exposed to messages that dictate how your body should seem, you may find yourself resorting to extreme methods in order to alter your body to conform to the perceived ideal body type. Habits, such as dieting, purging, or extreme exercise, are indicative of atypical anorexia and are often adopted to lose weight or prevent weight gain.

Atypical anorexia nervosa is a deceptive adversary, cleverly concealing itself among apparently healthy physiques. Originating from societal pressures and erroneous body images. This impactful book delves further, revealing the hidden challenges and highlighting the pressing necessity for awareness to help cultivate empathy and ignite transformation.

CHAPTER ONE

What is Anorexia?

Anorexia nervosa is a condition that affects a person's eating habits. This is a grave and potentially life-threatening mental health condition. Individuals with anorexia experience significant distress regarding their weight and body shape. They make a conscious effort to maintain a healthy weight by closely monitoring their diet. It is not uncommon for individuals with anorexia to engage in excessive exercise. They may also employ alternative approaches to manage their weight, such as utilizing laxatives, inducing vomiting post-meals, and resorting to stimulant drugs. Individuals suffering from anorexia, a grave mental illness, may restrict their food and beverage intake. They might establish guidelines regarding their dietary preferences, including their choices of food, as well as their preferred times and locations for meals.

Anorexia has the potential to impact individuals from all walks of life, regardless of their age, gender, ethnicity, or background. There are instances where anorexia nervosa may manifest as low body weight, but it is important to remember that one cannot accurately gauge someone's well-being based solely on their weight. Anorexia nervosa, commonly referred to as anorexia, is a recognized eating disorder. This condition causes an intense preoccupation with one's body weight and eating habits. If you are experiencing this issue, it is possible that you have an altered perception of your physical appearance. It may also be possible to perceive oneself as overweight despite having a significantly low body weight. When dealing with anorexia, individuals may adopt unconventional eating patterns as a means of managing stress, anxiety, and feelings of low self-worth. Restricting food intake can provide a feeling of empowerment in one's life. This issue has a greater impact on women compared to men. It typically begins in adolescence. Over the past years, there has been a consistent rise in the prevalence of anorexia nervosa among adolescent females aged 15 to 19.

Types of Anorexia

Restrictor Type: Individuals with this form of anorexia engage in a significant restriction of their food intake. Typically, this involves consuming foods that are rich in carbohydrates and fats.

Bulimic Type (Struggling with Binging and Purging): Individuals with bulimia engage in excessive food consumption followed by self-induced vomiting. Some individuals may resort to using various methods to cleanse their bowels, such as taking significant quantities of laxatives.

There is a higher likelihood of individuals with anorexia having a familial background with a history of specific health issues. Some of the issues that can arise are related to weight, physical health, and mental well-being. Some of the challenge individuals may face include feelings of sadness and struggles with substance abuse.

The treatment for anorexia nervosa usually requires a comprehensive approach that incorporates medical, nutritional, and psychological interventions. Psychotherapy, specifically cognitive-behavioral therapy (CBT), is frequently a crucial element of the treatment process. In certain instances, hospitalization may be required to address severe physical complications arising from malnutrition.

The perception of one's self-worth can be greatly influenced by factors such as weight and shape, particularly for individuals struggling with anorexia. Individuals may develop a habit of regularly monitoring their physical appearance and weight, or they may choose to steer clear of scales and mirrors. Individuals with anorexia may perceive themselves differently, often seeing themselves as larger than their actual size. This condition is commonly referred to as 'body dysmorphia'.

Psychological Characteristics of Anorexia

Severe physical problems can arise due to the effects of starvation on the body caused by anorexia. It may result in a decrease in muscle strength and bone strength. For some females, they may experience a cessation of their menstrual cycles, commonly referred to as 'amenorrhoea'. One may also notice a decrease in their sex drive. The illness may have consequences on individuals' relationships with their loved ones, leading them to become more isolated. Additionally, it can also affect their professional or academic pursuits.

Similar to other eating disorders, anorexia can be linked to feelings of sadness, a lack of confidence, unease, and additional complications or coexisting conditions. The gravity of the physical and emotional repercussions of the condition may not always be acknowledged or recognized, and individuals with anorexia may encounter challenges when seeking assistance – they may go to great extents to conceal their actions from loved ones, or at times may not even be aware of their illness. The psychological characteristics of anorexia in children and young people closely resemble those observed in adults. However, children and young people may exhibit lower weight, smaller stature, and slower physical development compared to their peers. There are several indications of anorexia, but it is not necessary for an individual to exhibit all of them in order to be experiencing the condition. Recognizing the presence of an eating disorder can sometimes be challenging, as they are classified as mental illnesses. If there are any concerns about yourself or someone else, it is advisable to promptly seek assistance. Acting swiftly increases the likelihood of a complete recovery.

CHAPTER TWO

Atypical Anorexia

When it comes to atypical anorexia, individuals meet all the criteria for anorexia nervosa, including restricting food and fluid and having a fear of gaining weight. However, their weight may not be significantly low, which is why it is referred to as "atypical." Those who are fortunate enough to receive a correct diagnosis of atypical anorexia nervosa are ideally referred to an outpatient team that specializes in treating eating disorders. An eating disorder known as atypical anorexia closely resembles anorexia. What sets them apart? Although individuals with anorexia may have significantly low body weights, those with atypical anorexia may weigh within the "normal" range or have larger bodies. Characterized as Other Specified Feeding or Eating Disorder (OSFED), atypical anorexia is commonly referred to as subthreshold anorexia. It is important to note that individuals of various genders, body types, and sizes can experience severe and potentially life-threatening complications as a result of atypical anorexia. Furthermore, there has been a noticeable increase in the number of individuals being diagnosed with atypical anorexia. Health concerns that would typically result in immediate medical attention for individuals who are underweight are downplayed for those with average or larger bodies. Some of the symptoms that may be observed are low/high heart rates and blood pressure, abnormal labs, dizziness, loss of vision, shortness of breath, fatigue, hair loss, and trouble sleeping.

There are few disparities in the impact of anorexia and atypical anorexia on individuals. The main distinction lies in the fact that individuals with anorexia exhibit a lower body weight to height ratio compared to those with atypical anorexia. Although there are similarities between the two eating disorders, those with atypical anorexia, who do not exhibit signs of being underweight, are less inclined to receive treatment for their eating disorder in comparison to those with anorexia who display visible signs of being underweight. Atypical anorexia exerts significant physical and mental control over an individual's daily life. If you suffer from an eating disorder, you may have an excessive preoccupation with thoughts related to food and body image. This may entail the practice of calorie counting and devising tactics to avoid social gatherings centered around food or having an unhealthy preoccupation with one's body weight. This can also impede various aspects of daily living, including as socializing, work efficiency, and maintaining relationships with friends and family. Individuals with atypical anorexia may also experience malnutrition-related medical or mental health complications, such as depression or anxiety.

Traits Associated with Atypical Anorexia

Individuals with preexisting mental health conditions such as anxiety, depression, bipolar disorder, or substance use may have an increased susceptibility to developing the unseen eating disorder, namely atypical anorexia. Additional characteristics strongly linked to atypical anorexia and other eating disorders include:

> The pursuit of perfection

> Inflexibility in cognitive processes or actions

> Diminished self-worth

- ➢ Issues related to personal relationships

- ➢ An account of past distressing experiences

- ➢ Difficulty in managing and controlling emotions

- ➢ Concerns related to one's perception and evaluation of their physical appearance.

If you identify with certain personality qualities mentioned, you might be more susceptible to developing an eating issue.

Eating disorders, like all mental health illnesses, have a biological basis.

Atypical anorexia, like to other eating disorders, is recognized to possess a significant hereditary correlation. If there is a history of eating disorders in your family, you are at a higher risk of developing an eating disorder yourself. However, it is important to clarify that parents should not be held responsible for a child's eating condition. Family support plays a crucial role in assisting individuals in overcoming eating problems. Exposure to social and cultural messages that promote a particular body type as superior to others is an additional risk factor for eating disorders. If you are constantly exposed to messages that dictate how your body should seem, you can resort to extreme methods in order to alter your body to conform to the perceived ideal body type. These habits, such as dieting, purging, or extreme exercise, are indicative of atypical anorexia and are often adopted to lose weight or prevent weight gain. Vulnerable persons can be exposed to these social and cultural messages through several means:

- Acquaintances, relatives, mentors, dance instructors, or other individuals

- Online platforms, periodicals, television, and films

- Social media applications, where the use of Photoshop, filters, and photo manipulation is widespread.

- Famous individuals and influential figures in the realm of physical fitness

- Communication originating from companies in the diet and weight-loss sector.

Individuals of diverse age groups and genders can be subjected to these signals, hence heightening the susceptibility to developing eating problems.

Engaging in sports offers young individuals an excellent opportunity to engage in physical activity, interact with others, and cultivate a positive sense of self-worth. Nevertheless, all sports have the potential to heighten the susceptibility to developing eating problems, regardless of gender. Pursuing the ideal athletic physique or striving to enhance performance through intensified training and dietary modifications can give rise to ideas and actions associated with eating disorders.

Implementing dietary restrictions to reduce caloric consumption such as engaging in excessive consumption of food followed by purging, which may involve inducing vomiting, using laxatives, or employing other methods.

Engaging in excessive exercise such as running several miles every day even while injured : Certain athletic coaches and dance teachers persist in promoting weight reduction in young athletes, employing any methods deemed necessary. Despite the potential health consequences and negative impact on athletic performance, this detrimental behavior persists.

CHAPTER THREE

Unusual Manifestations of

Anorexia Nervosa

Individuals with atypical anorexia nervosa may resort to extensive measures to hide their eating condition or assert that they no longer limit their food consumption when faced with persistent inquiries regarding their eating habits. Furthermore, mental health disorders such as depression, anxiety, or OCD can intensify this denial. Individuals with one of these conditions have a significantly higher likelihood of experiencing an eating disorder. It is rather typical for eating disorders to occur alongside other disorders.

Like other eating disorders, atypical anorexia can cause various mental health consequences and may contribute to the development of other psychiatric disorders. The distinction between typical and atypical anorexia nervosa lies in their weight, as individuals with typical anorexia nervosa do not often exhibit significant weight reduction. As a result, numerous behavioral and emotional indicators might be likened. Nevertheless, it is important to note a significant differentiation: individuals with atypical anorexia may really perceive themselves as being in a satisfactory state or may erroneously assume that their weight eliminates any potential hazards associated with their behaviors. If an individual is not significantly underweight, their disorder may remain undetected.

Individuals suffering from anorexia nervosa often vehemently reject the notion that they are significantly underweight or that they are afflicted with an eating disorder. Typically, individuals with atypical anorexia nervosa exhibit a tendency to deny the presence of an eating problem or acknowledge the detrimental impact of their eating patterns on their overall well-being. Individuals with atypical anorexia nervosa may respond to their eating disorder by downplaying its effects on their health, accusing family and friends of unjustly targeting them for a non-existent issue, or attributing their eating disorder to external factors such as relationships or job-related stress.

The signs of atypical anorexia closely resemble those of anorexia nervosa, including a considerable reduction in daily caloric intake and the adoption of weight-avoidance strategies such as dieting, fasting, or extreme exercise. Individuals with atypical anorexia may exhibit many mental health problems, such as:

> Obesophobia is a profound dread of weight growth or of having a bigger physique.

> An intense desire to alter your weight, physical size, or shape, regardless of the consequences.

> Discontentment with physical dimensions, configuration, or overall look, an altered perception of one's body or body dysmorphic disorder

- Diminished self-worth, fluctuating emotions, and feelings of unease or despondency
- Difficulty maintaining concentration or attention
- Tiredness
- Contemplation of suicide or engaging in self-inflicted damage

A significant number of individuals with atypical anorexia hold the belief that they do not require treatment due to their lack of being underweight, as they perceive themselves as not being sufficiently ill. However, the reduction in body weight or prolonged limitation of calorie intake linked to atypical anorexia might lead to severe complications.

Indicators to Monitor

If you or someone you are concerned about is excessively focused on food, body weight, size, or shape, or exhibits abnormal eating patterns, it is advisable to consider seeking assistance from a qualified professional to address a potential eating disorder. If you or someone you know is suffering from this condition, then these indications of atypical anorexia would be recognizable.

- Heightened irritation, diminished self-esteem, or fluctuating moods

- Omitting meals or refraining from communal eating

- Excessively fixating on nutrition labels or calorie counts

- Adhering to dietary restrictions by excluding specific foods or food categories

- Engaging in episodes of excessive eating as a means of numbing distressing feelings

- Difficulty in managing and controlling emotions

- Regularly monitoring one's weight or frequently examining one's body in mirrors

Individuals with atypical anorexia may exhibit no discernible physical symptoms. Nevertheless, despite the absence of physical symptoms, the individual may nevertheless experience mental distress.

CHAPTER FOUR

Difficulties Posed by Atypical

Anorexia

Atypical anorexia is classified as a mental health illness and is relatively little acknowledged or comprehended compared to the more prevalent eating disorders. A significant number of individuals with atypical anorexia fail to meet the established criteria for anorexia nervosa, hence complicating the process of obtaining appropriate treatment. They may also persistently experience the physical and psychological consequences of their eating disorder for an extended duration.

An additional concern about atypical anorexia is its increased difficulty in early-stage detection. Individuals diagnosed with atypical anorexia may not consistently exhibit significantly low body weight, in contrast to individuals with anorexia nervosa, where low body weight is a primary diagnostic criterion. Their dietary patterns may also be less regulated and unpredictable, hence complicating the diagnosis of the disease. Moreover, individuals may not have an equivalent level of preoccupation with food, weight, or body form as persons with anorexia nervosa, thereby complicating the process of diagnosis. Therefore, it is crucial to be cognizant of supplementary unconventional anorexia signs such as apprehension regarding weight increase, a distorted image of one's body, and excessive physical exertion.

Moreover, individuals with atypical anorexia are frequently motivated by an intense dread of weight gain and obesity, which influences their behavior. Typically, individuals with this illness have significantly higher levels of distress related to eating and have a distorted sense of their body image, in comparison to those who do not have the disorder.

The condition of atypical anorexia often goes unrecognized in families, schools, and healthcare settings. Moreover, these individuals are frequently commended for their weight loss and restrictive behaviors. Compliments regarding their physical appearance and commitment to maintaining good health are given when they begin to consume less food or alter their dietary habits.

These responses bolster the unhealthy eating patterns, so reinforcing the beliefs about one's value and physical appearance, as well as the anxieties related to gaining weight. In addition, individuals may also encounter specialists who provide them with invalidating information, such as prescribing weight loss drugs or attributing their pain or medical issues only to their larger weight.

Due to the common association of "thin" with "healthy," crucial chances to detect, confront, and manage eating problems frequently go unnoticed. Nevertheless, persons with atypical anorexia who are at greater weights experience a simultaneous deterioration of organ function over time, similar to patients diagnosed with the more prevalent form of anorexia.

Adverse Effects of Atypical Anorexia

The physical problems linked to atypical anorexia are equally severe as those associated with anorexia. Individuals with atypical anorexia, who engage in dietary restriction, are susceptible to many severe complications, which may include:

- Bradycardia refers to an unusually low heartbeat.
- Hypotension
- Osteoporosis

- ➤ Fluctuations in hormones or disorders related to the reproductive system
- ➤ Delayed healing injuries or stress fractures
- ➤ Tiredness
- ➤ Gastrointestinal disorder

Significantly, the medical state of those with atypical anorexia can be equally severe, if not more so, than individuals with anorexia. Individuals with atypical anorexia may not exhibit a low body mass index (BMI), but if they rapidly lose a substantial amount of weight or engage in prolonged calorie restriction, they might nonetheless suffer from symptoms of malnutrition. Malnutrition can manifest regardless of an individual's physical weight, despite common misconceptions.

Possible causes of malnutrition include:

- Following a highly limited dietary regimen

- Shedding a substantial amount of weight, regardless of whether you are still within or above the "normal" body mass index (BMI) range.

- Engaging in prolonged calorie deprivation, especially in cases where your body has shown resistance to losing weight

Indicators of malnutrition to be vigilant about include:

- Tiredness Lack of strength

- Difficulty maintaining focus

- Vertigo

- Insufficient levels of vitamins

Regardless of whether you are not clinically underweight, any quick or substantial reduction in weight might result in severe medical consequences. Fortunately, eating disorder treatment can effectively alleviate a significant number of the physical health problems commonly linked to atypical anorexia. Due to the absence of visible emaciation in persons with atypical anorexia, healthcare providers are less inclined to recommend eating disorder treatment for these patients.

Consequently, individuals with atypical anorexia, particularly those with larger body weights, may not receive the necessary and rightful assistance. A matter of significant concern is that individuals with atypical anorexia nervosa may be susceptible to bradyarrhythmia, which increases the likelihood of premature mortality. Atypical anorexia is correlated with an increase in suicidal ideation.

CHAPTER FIVE

Treatment for Atypical Anorexia

Treatment for atypical anorexia employs a range of strategies to assist individuals in overcoming ideas and behaviors associated with eating disorders. The treatment team members cooperate to offer medical and dietary assistance, individual counseling, group counseling, family counseling, and additional services.

Medical Intervention

Patients diagnosed with atypical anorexia may need initial medical stabilization to address any lingering medical issues. Upon your arrival for treatment, the treatment team will promptly conduct laboratory tests to evaluate the presence of nutritional symptoms. Medical physicians and psychiatrists oversee and provide assistance to individuals who are experiencing severe illness. Psychotropic drugs and other pharmaceuticals are provided to facilitate the process of recovery. Nursing experts collaborate closely with the treatment team to manage the consequences associated with atypical anorexia, administering medical care in cases requiring emergency intervention.

Psychotherapy

Psychotherapy is a crucial component of the comprehensive treatment for atypical anorexia. Skilled clinicians specializing in eating disorders provide individualized treatment to patients, utilizing various evidence-based therapy strategies to facilitate behavioral transformation. Therapists teach patients coping mechanisms and encourage them to overcome harmful cognitive processes. Atypical anorexia treatment incorporates evidence-based interventions such as:

- Acceptance and Commitment Therapy (ACT)

- Cognitive Behavioral Therapy (CBT)

- Dialectical Behavioral Therapy (DBT)

- Radically Open Dialectical Behavior Therapy (RO DBT)

Exposure therapy

Therapy also addresses co-morbid mental health issues, such as anxiety, depression, bipolar disorder, and others.

Therapeutic group sessions

Group therapy is an essential element of the treatment for atypical anorexia.

Group therapy provides patients with both peer and professional support while they acquire the skills to address and rectify detrimental eating and activity patterns, rigid dietary regulations, and detrimental thoughts and behaviors associated with eating disorders. Patients receive instruction in recovery methods and relapse prevention techniques while simultaneously addressing body acceptance and body image concerns. The eating disorder treatment approach also integrates experiential treatments such as art, psychodrama, mindfulness, movement, and yoga.

Therapy that focuses on the dynamics and relationships within a family unit.

An essential aspect of treating atypical anorexia is adopting a family-centered approach. Family members and other individuals in the support system have a significant impact on an individual's recovery at all stages of life. Family-Based Treatment and Emotion Focused Family therapy enables parents, partners, and other individuals to actively facilitate positive transformation for their loved ones, providing them with the necessary support to maintain lasting healing.

Family treatment involves providing education to parents, spouses, family members, and loved ones to enhance their comprehension of the consequences of atypical anorexia and strategies for overcoming the eating problem.

Telemedicine

The emerging discipline of virtual eating disorder treatment offers a flexible alternative for treating atypical anorexia, enabling clients to get guidance from professional treatment providers without leaving their homes. Experts in virtual eating disorder therapy offer evidence-based dietary assistance and therapeutic intervention. Interventions in virtual treatment closely resemble the therapeutic options mentioned in this list.

Recovery from Atypical Anorexia

While atypical anorexia nervosa is classified as an eating disorder, individuals in recovery from anorexia nervosa typically do not exhibit visible indications of severe medical consequences commonly associated with other eating disorders. This does not imply that the health risks are diminished; it just means that the individual has not been classified as underweight by their doctors. Experts in the field of eating disorder treatment are knowledgeable about this particular variation, however. Hence, anorexia nervosa treatment clinics frequently conduct blood and urine tests to ascertain whether any underlying health issues must be attended to prior to commencing psychiatric therapy.

Upon commencing treatment for atypical anorexia, individuals are provided with comprehensive medical, nutritional, and psychosocial support by seasoned eating disorder specialists. Groups, community meetings, nutritional support, and individual treatment all contribute to the individual's rehabilitation by:

- Tackling the physiological consequences and medical complexities

- Assisting patients in resuming their normal dietary habits and routines

- Enhancing psychological well-being, physical appearance, and emotional state

During the treatment process, the patient is provided with a personalized eating disorder treatment plan that prioritizes the development of skills to facilitate recovery post-treatment. Upon the completion of treatment, aftercare planning and alumni services are implemented to ensure a systematic and uninterrupted continuation of care, thereby preserving the progress achieved throughout therapy.

CHAPTER SIX

Treatment for Eating Disorders in Individuals with Elevated Body Mass

Healthcare professionals are more inclined to recommend persons with noticeably low body weights for eating disorder treatment. In contrast, individuals with atypical anorexia, who may have weights that are considered "normal" or higher, may not receive a referral for treatment, even though they experience various medical and mental health complications. This highlights the necessity of providing education to healthcare personnel regarding atypical anorexia and the gravity of the condition, irrespective of the patient's weight during assessment or their weight history. Prioritizing the prompt intervention for restricting attitudes and behaviors is crucial to prevent the exacerbation of the illness and the intensification of medical consequences.

Restoration of optimal nutrition

After achieving medical stability, a primary objective of treatment will be to reintegrate conventional eating patterns in order to restore normal eating behaviors and food consumption.

Patients often have consultations with registered nutritionists as part of their treatment for atypical anorexia. Mealtime support is overseen by behavioral health counselors to accommodate patients who may have anxiety or reluctance to eat throughout therapy. Registered dietitians and clinicians are accessible on an as-needed basis. Instruction is given on food portions, food presentation, and the basic principles of nutrition.

Enhanced awareness regarding the consequences of atypical anorexia and its indicators would enable us to provide assistance to afflicted individuals at an earlier stage. This results in a decreased prevalence rate, reduced utilization of the healthcare system, and a lower number of fatalities. Clinicians evaluating and managing eating disorders should not make the assumption that persons with atypical anorexia are healthier than those with normal anorexia, or that malnourishment can only occur in those with a smaller body size. Furthermore, it is crucial to be cognizant of the communication we are conveying to those with higher body weights in relation to weight and well-being. The size of an individual's physique does not exclude them from the requirement to reduce calorie intake and/or achieve weight loss. Contemporary eating disorder treatment programs now focus on evaluating if patients have nutritional consequences caused by their condition, independent of their initial BMI.

By developing a comprehensive comprehension of eating disorders, including both typical and atypical manifestations, we can effectively minimize the frequency and length of people's suffering, enabling them to swiftly achieve a state of well-being.

Insufficient awareness on atypical anorexia nervosa may hinder parents and teenagers from participating in anorexia recovery programs. The absence of weight loss is not the determining factor for atypical anorexia nervosa, while the symptoms of anorexia nervosa are generally mostly same. There is significant similarity between the two eating disorders, and it is important to exercise caution when being diagnosed with either of them. The importance of treatment should not be disregarded just based on the absence of a medically underweight condition in an individual. This is a useful guideline for all eating problems. BMI and other weight metrics do not necessarily reflect a person's emotional or physical well-being. Eating disorder rehabilitation programs prioritize mindfulness, nutritional and intuitive eating, and the restoration of a person's body image, rather than fixating on their weight.

If an individual is exhibiting obsessive-compulsive behaviors related to food restriction, calorie counting, fat gram counting, or engaging in ritualistic food activities during meals, and they are not below a healthy weight, it is advisable for them to undergo evaluation by specialists who are skilled in identifying indications of an eating disorder. Commencing this initial phase promptly is crucial for achieving a complete recuperation.

Individuals battling atypical anorexia negotiate not only their personal conflicts but also cultural biases that can exacerbate their challenges. By breaking the bias via education, spreading compassionate language, and cultivating understanding, society can become an ally rather than an adversary. It is time to adopt a narrative that promotes empathy, facilitates open communication, and supports the holistic well-being of persons afflicted by atypical anorexia.

END